SMART ABOUT SPORTS

Meet the Vikings

By
Mike Kennedy
with Mark Stewart

NORWOOD HOUSE PRESS

Norwood House Press, P.O. Box 316598, Chicago, Illinois 60631

For information regarding Norwood House Press,
please visit our website at: www.norwoodhousepress.com or call 866-565-2900.

Photo Credits:
  Getty Images (4, 7, 8, 12, 13, 15, 16, 20, 21), Black Book Partners (18, 23), Associated Press (22).
Cover Photos:
  Top Left: The Upper Deck Company; Top Right: Tim Steadman/Icon SMI;
  Bottom Left: Jack Rendulich/Icon SMI; Bottom Right: Donruss Playoff LP.
The football memorabilia photographed for this book is part of the authors' collection:
  Page 6) Mick Tingelhoff: Topps, Inc., Page 10) Fran Tarkenton: The Upper Deck Company; Jim Marshall:
  Sunoco, Inc.; Alan, Page & Carl Eller: Topps, Inc., Page 11) Paul Krause: Topps, Inc.; John Randle: NFL Pro Set;
  Adrian Peterson: Donruss Playoff LP; Cris Carter: The Upper Deck Company.
Special thanks to Topps, Inc.

Editor: Brian Fitzgerald
Designer: Ron Jaffe
Project Management: Black Book Partners, LLC.
Editorial Production: Jessica McCulloch

LIBRARY OF CONGRESS CATALOGING-IN-PUBLICATION DATA
    Kennedy, Mike, 1965-
    Meet the Vikings / by Mike Kennedy with Mark Stewart.
        p. cm. -- (Smart about sports)
    Includes bibliographical references and index.
    Summary: "An introductory look at the Minnesota Vikings football team.
    Includes a brief history, facts, photos, records, glossary, and fun
    activities"--Provided by publisher.
    ISBN-13: 978-1-59953-398-8 (library edition : alk. paper)
    ISBN-10: 1-59953-398-7 (library edition : alk. paper)
    1. Minnesota Vikings (Football team)--History--Juvenile literature. I.
    Stewart, Mark, 1960- II. Title.
    GV956.M5K46 2011
    796.332'6409776579--dc22

                        2010005805

Manufactured in the United States of America in North Mankato, Minnesota.
156N–072010

Contents

Words in **bold type** are defined on page 24.

The Vikings run onto the field.

The Minnesota Vikings

Vikings lived a long time ago. They were strong and tough. Minnesota's football team is named after them. The players and fans have the Viking spirit.

Once Upon a Time

Mick
TINGELHOFF
MINNESOTA VIKINGS • CENTER

The Vikings joined the National Football League (NFL) in 1961. The Vikings have always put great players on the field. Mick Tingelhoff and Fran Tarkenton were two of the best.

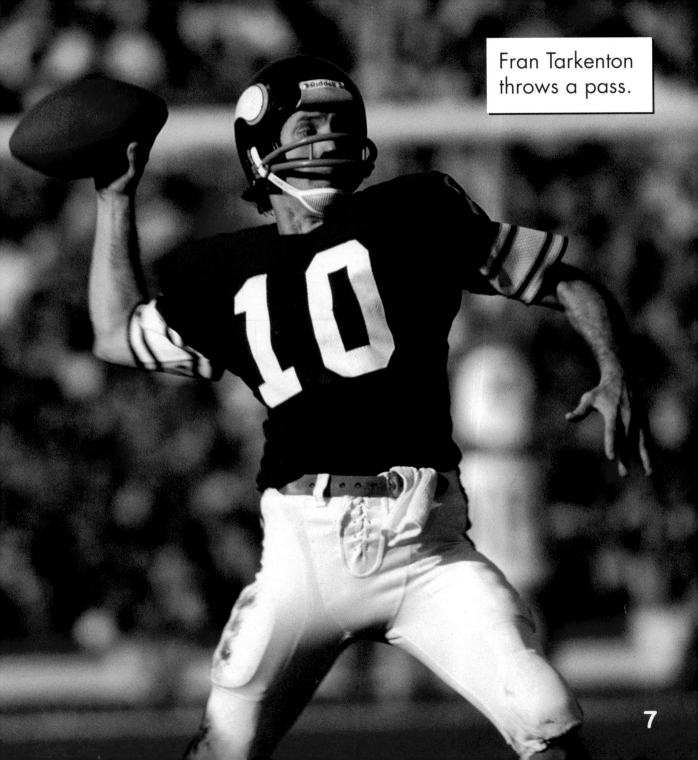

Fran Tarkenton throws a pass.

Fans fill the Metrodome for a 2009 game.

At the Stadium

The Vikings play their home games at the Hubert H. Humphrey Metrodome. It is a big stadium with a large roof. The players like the stadium. Their fans can get very loud.

Shoe Box

The cards on these pages belong to the authors. They show some of the best Vikings ever.

Fran Tarkenton

Quarterback
- 1961–1966 & 1972–1978
Fran Tarkenton was very quick. Tacklers had a hard time catching him.

Jim Marshall

Defensive Lineman
- 1961–1979
Jim Marshall led Minnesota's defense for 19 years.

70 Jim Marshall DE
Minnesota Vikings

Carl Eller

Defensive Lineman
- 1964–1978
Carl Eller stopped offenses from running and passing.

CARL ELLER

DEFENSIVE END
VIKINGS

Alan Page

Defensive Lineman
- 1967–1978
Alan Page forced many quarterbacks to make bad throws.

VIKINGS NFC
DEFENSIVE TACKLE
ALAN PAGE

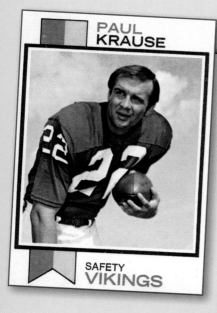

Paul Krause

Safety • 1968–1979
Paul Krause had the most **interceptions** in NFL history.

John Randle

Defensive Lineman • 1990–2000
John Randle was one of the best at tackling quarterbacks.

Cris Carter

Receiver • 1990–2001
Cris Carter scored 110 **touchdowns** for the team.

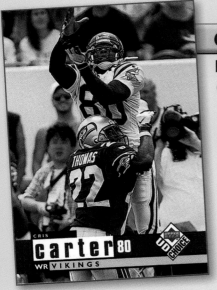

Adrian Peterson

Running Back • 2007–
Adrian Peterson ran with power and speed.

ABC's
of
Football

Look at this picture of Percy Harvin. How many things can you find that start with the letter **S**?

See page 23 for answer.

13

Brain Games

Here is a poem about a famous Viking:

There once was a Viking named Chuck.
He ran with the force of a truck.
He made lots of catches,
Scored touchdowns in batches.
To stop him took both skill and luck.

Guess which one of these facts is **TRUE**:

- *Chuck Foreman led the NFL in catches in 1975.*

- *Chuck's real name is Charles.*

See page 23 for answer.

14

Chuck Foreman looks for an opening in the defense.

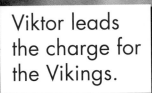

Viktor leads the charge for the Vikings.

Fun on the Field

The Vikings have two mascots. Viktor looks like a cartoon Viking. Ragnar is a man dressed like a Viking. Both love to have fun and cheer with the fans.

On the Map

The Vikings call Minneapolis, Minnesota home. The players come from all over the world. These Vikings played in the **Pro Bowl**. Match each with the place he was born:

 Bill Brown • Pro Bowl: 1964–1965 & 1967–1968
Mendota, Illinois

 Mick Tingelhoff • Pro Bowl: 1964–1969
Lexington, Nebraska

 Tommy Kramer
• Pro Bowl: 1986
San Antonio, Texas

 Randall McDaniel
• Pro Bowl: 1989–2000
Phoenix, Arizona

 Fuad Reveiz • Pro Bowl: 1994
Bogota, Colombia

The Vikings play
in Minneapolis, Minnesota.

19

What's in the Locker?

The team's home uniform has a purple shirt with wide white stripes. The Vikings also use flashes of gold.

Sidney Rice wears the team's home uniform.

The team's road uniform has a white jersey with purple and gold stripes. The team always wears a purple helmet. It has horns like the ones old-time Vikings wore.

Chad Greenway wears the team's road uniform.

We Won!

The Vikings won the NFL title in 1969.
Coach Bud Grant built a strong team. The
team's defense
was great. It
was called
the "Purple
People Eaters."

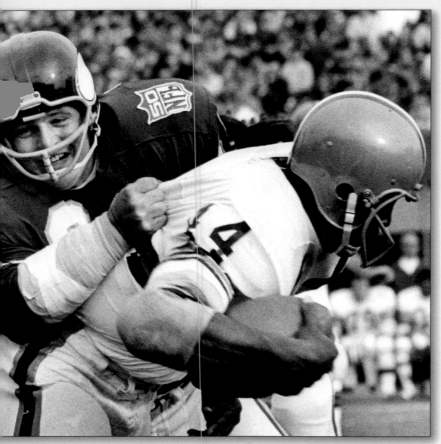

Roy Winston makes a
tackle for the Vikings.

Record Book

These Vikings stars set team records.

Running Back	Record	Year
Chuck Foreman	22 total touchdowns	1975
Adrian Peterson	1,760 **yards**	2008

Quarterback/Receiver	Record	Year
Cris Carter*	122 catches	1994
Randy Moss	1,632 receiving yards	2003
Daunte Culpepper	39 touchdown passes	2004

* Carter also had 122 catches in 1995.

Answer for ABC's of Football

Here are some words in the picture that start with S: Shoe, Shoulder Pad, Sock.
Did you find any others?

Answer for Brain Games

The first fact is true. Chuck Foreman caught 73 passes in 1975. "Chuck" is short for Charles. But this Chuck's real name is Walter.

Football Words

INTERCEPTIONS
Passes caught by the defense.

PRO BOWL
A special game played between the NFL's top stars.

TOUCHDOWNS
Scoring plays worth six points.

YARDS
A yard is a distance of three feet. A football field is 100 yards from goal line to goal line.

Index

Photos are on **bold** numbered pages.

About the Vikings

Learn more about the Vikings at www.vikings.com
Learn more about football at www.profootballhof.com